PHRESH
PHARMACY

New ideas for the business of community pharmacy

By Meyada Widaatalla

PharmD, BCGP

I dedicate this book to my parents

Contents

Introduction

I like the rush of community pharmacy- it's energizing. When I sit alone at a desk I get bored and can easily fall asleep. But constantly being on my feet, answering phone calls, acknowledging customers on the other side of the counter - I'd be lucky if I could close my eyes for 10 seconds.

Sometimes it's too much. Sometimes I just want a few minutes in my shift to eat, call family or do my daily prayers.

When I'm the only pharmacist working a shift, it is both gratifying and frustrating to be needed so much by the team. I'm sure any community pharmacist reading this knows the feeling of guilt to just step out of the floor for a minute to take a breath of fresh air, grab a bite of delicious lemon cranberry muffin or check messages. The feeling of anxiety that someone will call your name soon and the mini-break you allowed yourself will be over. And to anyone reading this who is the customer on the other side of the counter: we are not just playing around when we say your prescription requires 30 minutes of preparation time. That is truly the best time we can offer.

The scope of practice for community pharmacists is expanding. Pharmacist jobs are becoming more clinically focused rather than technically focused. It's all very exciting, but is the business environment we currently practice in *ready* for this change? Is the infrastructure there to help the already overwhelmed pharmacist complete clinical tasks? My personal opinion is no. In this book, I offer some practical and ideal solutions to help make the retail pharmacy work environment ready for these changes. I hope to offer fresh, new ideas to policymakers, pharmacy stakeholders, pharmacy managers and owners. But mostly, I want to empower the community pharmacist to step back from the counter, look up from the constant stream of scripts and ask yourself: what changes would make my job easier and more enjoyable? Just because we are busy it doesn't mean we don't want to see change or have ideas on how change can happen. And we shouldn't wait for those in administrative or corporate positions to decide what will happen and when. It is up to us.

Background : Community Pharmacy in Ontario, Canada

Every pharmacy is a unique business with a specific clientele, workflow, and staff. Since most of my experience has been in community pharmacies in Ontario, Canada, I will describe the general working environment and current pharmacist scope of practice in Ontario in this section. I aim to provide the reader with a background to understand the issues and potential solutions that will be discussed later on. Of course, the issues and solutions in this book are not only applicable to Ontario pharmacies.

I use the terms retail pharmacy and community pharmacy interchangeably throughout the book.

Pharmacist tasks in the dispensary

New prescriptions and refills are generally ordered via one of three ways: phone, fax or by the patient delivering the physical prescription itself. Even when a pharmacy is closed overnight there are still new prescriptions and refills being ordered as the fax machine and voicemail on pharmacy phones are usually still operating. The opening pharmacy team has to check messages and input orders that came in overnight, address any outstanding issues from the day before, open the narcotic safe and prepare workstations. If that's not bad enough, remember the phones will start ringing and patients coming in through the door when the pharmacy officially opens or shortly after that. If you have ever wondered why retail pharmacists are on their feet and not sitting down, it's because there is always some kind of interruption the pharmacist has to attend to. This can be a question from a patient about an over-the-counter product, a patient who is picking up a new prescription and requires counselling, a drug representative who would like to speak to the pharmacist about a new product, a physician or prescriber who would like to order a prescription verbally, or an inventory order that has to be signed by the pharmacist before being received or sent off. Interruptions are a huge barrier between pharmacists and their job fulfillment and completion of thorough clinical tasks. This will be discussed later on in the book.

The three main income generators in retail pharmacies are prescriptions (which are each charged a dispensing fee aside from the cost of the drug), over-the-counter sales, and professional or clinical services. The most popular professional services within the scope of practice of Ontario pharmacists are medication reviews (also known as MedsChecks), immunizations, Pharmaceutical Opinions (interventions the pharmacist communicates to the prescriber when there is a prescription error), and Smoking Cessation consultations. Pharmacists in Ontario have also recently been granted the authority to prescribe for several minor ailments. These clinical services have restrictions regarding who can and cannot receive them, how they should be documented, where they are provided and for what length of time. These restrictions exist because the government wants to ensure that they are quality services that benefit taxpayers.

MedsChecks can be completed for patients who have provincial health benefits and are on three or more chronic medications. There are several pages of documentation to be completed by the pharmacist and some pages have to be faxed to the patient's family physician while other pages are signed and given to the patient. They are reimbursed $25-$150 each depending on the type of MedsCheck (annual, follow-up, diabetes or at home). MedsChecks are expected to be completed in a private area with the length of the interaction being at least 20 minutes (Ontario Ministry of Health 2023). In many cases, however, employers and the tight workflow pressure pharmacists to complete Medschecks in 10 minutes or less right at the pharmacy counter, while also completing their primary task of checking prescriptions. There is often a conflict of interest in retail pharmacy because the pharmacist is the one responsible for making ethical clinical decisions in the interest of the patient and selling medications or clinical services to that patient. Pharmacies make more money by checking more prescriptions and providing more services, regardless of the quality of those services or whether or not patients need them. It can therefore be very overwhelming for pharmacists to check prescriptions and complete professional services properly when there is a business obligation to make more money.

How prescriptions are processed

The usual workflow of a retail pharmacy is as follows:

1) The patient brings in a prescription (or the prescription is faxed in or phoned directly to the pharmacist on duty by the prescriber).

2) The prescription is entered into the pharmacy software by a staff member (usually a pharmacy assistant or technician). All details are entered under the patient's profile including drug name, dosage, and quantity (plus any

refills) and the prescription is processed through the patient's insurance plan(s), if applicable.

Note the difference between a pharmacy assistant and a pharmacy technician- a technician is a regulated health professional who has undergone specific pharmacy-related training in college and, like pharmacists, is licensed under a regulatory body (e.g. the Ontario College of Pharmacists). An assistant has not necessarily undergone any pharmacy-related training in college/ university and is not licensed or regulated. Pharmacy assistants help with the technical aspects of the pharmacy workflow but unlike pharmacy technicians, they are not authorized to perform technical checks.

3) A label is printed with all patient and drug details. The label moves to the filling station where the drug is prepared and labelled.

4) The prepared medication is sent to the checking station where a technical and clinical check are performed. The technical check assesses whether the drug was prepared correctly (e.g. correct quantity dispensed, labelled correctly for the right patient, expiration dates etc.). The clinical check assesses whether the drug is an appropriate choice for the patient and whether it has been prescribed correctly (e.g. no serious drug interactions with other drugs on file, the patient doesn't have any allergies to the medication, the dose is appropriate etc.). The clinical check must be completed by a pharmacist and the technical check can be completed by a regulated pharmacy technician. When a pharmacy technician is not available, the pharmacist must complete both the technical and clinical checks.

5) The medication is put into a bag and the bag is labelled with the patient's name and identi-

fier (e.g. date of birth, address and/or tele-
phone number).

6) The bag is placed either in the pickup area or
the fridge (if the medication requires refriger-
ation).

7) When the patient picks up their prescription,
they will pay any applicable charges and the
pharmacist can (with the patient's consent)
provide counselling if the medication is new
to ensure it is used properly and that any
drug-related concerns are addressed.

It is important to note that this is the order of
steps in most cases. I have worked in a pharmacy
where the pharmacist performs a clinical check before the prescription is prepared. The order of steps
is not necessarily as listed above although, at some
point in a pharmacy's workflow, all the steps above
are completed.

Also, note that staffing can vary greatly from one
pharmacy to the next. Unfortunately, not all pharma-

cies have regulated pharmacy technicians to help with technical checks. The majority of pharmacies I have worked in don't have a regulated pharmacy technician - only pharmacists and pharmacy assistants. Depending on the pharmacy's daily script count, there may be more than one pharmacist on duty. For example, I once worked at a retail pharmacy that filled 300 or more prescriptions daily and another pharmacy that filled less than 100 scripts per day. The former always had two staff pharmacists overlapping their shifts during busy hours from 12 pm to 5 pm whereas the latter pharmacy had one staff pharmacist working the full 9-hour day. The clientele can also vary greatly. Some pharmacies are located within medical buildings and mostly serve patients whose physicians are in the same building or those who attend a walk-in clinic in the building. Other pharmacies are not near any particular prescriber and serve anyone in the public.

In addition, patients are allowed to choose which pharmacies they dispense their medications at. If I am a patient on rosuvastatin for cholesterol, amlodipine for blood pressure and insulin for diabetes, I could have each of these three medications dispensed at three different pharmacies. Furthermore, pharmacy systems are not interconnected and pharmacies don't magically communicate with one another. You would be surprised how many people don't know this. For confidentiality reasons, Pharmacy A doesn't have access to the patient profiles and medication lists that Pharmacy B next door has on file. Even if Pharmacies A and B are in the same company (e.g. Walmart, Costco, Shoppers Drug Mart), Pharmacy A has no idea what the patients going to Pharmacy B are taking. Most patients have one primary pharmacy where they get all or most of their medications dispensed. However, having even one or two medications dispensed elsewhere means they would have an incomplete record at their primary pharmacy. This makes it harder for the pharmacist to do a proper clinical check.

Although workflow, staffing and clientele vary between pharmacies, all retail pharmacies prepare medications and provide clinical services that help to address issues with these medications.

Why the community pharmacy work environment has to change

Retail pharmacies in Ontario have recently been provided access to digital health information for their patients (Ontario College of Pharmacists 2021). This information is important for performing clinical checks and includes lab results, past medical history and medication history. In every province in Canada and generally throughout North America, the scope of practice for retail pharmacists is expanding. This is to support a more clinical role for the pharmacist. Before entering pharmacy school, the university I attended offered a Bachelor of Science in Pharmacy (BScPhm) program. It now only offers the entry-to-practice Doctor of Pharmacy (PharmD) program which is more clinically focused compared to the previous BScPhm. Faculties of pharmacy have adopted this newer degree program because the role of the pharmacist in our societies has changed from dispensing medications to being directly involved in the care of patients. In this book, I argue that the current work environment in most retail pharmacies does not support the clinical role pharmacists are expected to fulfill. The retail pharmacy work environment must change for two very important reasons:

1. to support a more clinical role for pharmacists, and

2. to ensure job satisfaction for pharmacists.

Allowing pharmacists to perform more clinical services for their patients without solving underlying workflow and business model issues will only make pharmacists more overwhelmed. Pharmacists are the most accessible healthcare professionals but they are among the least satisfied. According to a survey, 7 out of 10 pharmacists are not happy with their jobs (Barrett 2020). Ironically, there has never been a more exciting time to be a pharmacist because big change is happening in our profession. We just can't enjoy these changes yet. Several barriers must be addressed first.

Part 2:

The Barriers and Their Practical Solutions

Chapter 1:

Barrier 1: Lack of time

The Problem

According to a study conducted on community pharmacists in the UK, lack of time was the number one cause of moral distress on the job (Robinson 2019). Pharmacists are not fully satisfied with their jobs because they don't have enough time to do their jobs properly. Isn't that unfortunate? Most people complain of bad bosses or co-workers, or lack of recognition for their hard work. All pharmacists want is more time.

The cause of the problem

In most cases there is only one pharmacist on duty and that one pharmacist has hundreds of prescriptions to check and numerous non-stop interruptions to deal with. By law, it is required that every prescription leaving a pharmacy must have been reviewed by the pharmacist. But there are too many prescriptions for just one pharmacist. One article from Drug Topics states: 'Chain stores often require pharmacists to dispense 300 or more [prescriptions] a day. That's 37.5 prescriptions an hour in an 8-hour shift or 1.6 minutes per prescription, during which time a pharmacist must verify the accuracy of the label, check the patient profile for duplications/ interactions, contact prescribers if any issues arise, call the insurer as needed, verify that the contents of the prescription vial are accurate, and counsel the patient on the medication - impossible!' (Drug Topics 2015). There is no way that 1.6 minutes is enough time for a thorough check of all possible drug-related problems, let alone fixing any issues before they reach the patient. Even if a pharmacist is just performing a technical check for the correct patient, correct drug, and correct quantity, this would not be enough time. What if there is an error? In my experience, it takes at least 10 minutes to amend errors considering the correct information has to be inputted and processed again through the pharmacy software, a new label printed and the packaging re-done and checked with this new label. Of course, no one is timing the pharmacist to make sure each script is checked in exactly a certain number of minutes, but there is always a sense of urgency in retail pharmacy and not completing prescription checks in a very short amount of time will create delays and unhappy customers.

Furthermore, clinical interventions can only be addressed by the pharmacist. Clinical interventions are not part of the scope of practice of other pharmacy staff members. This means the pharmacist alone is the one responsible for taking most prescriber phone calls, answering most over-the-counter product questions and counselling patients. There is very limited time to complete each prescription check and each patient encounter. Many pharmacists, myself included, want to spend more time counselling their patients (Gebhart 2019) and consulting references to do more research on certain topics. But we simply don't have the time to do this as we are constantly being pulled away from one task to another, always expecting to be interrupted.

One of the things that always bothers me is when I have finally checked a pile of prescriptions and want to pause for a few minutes to take a closer look at a patient's medication profile or research a drug question and when I look up there is suddenly a whole new stack of baskets to check. Where did they all come from? I can't help but remember how lucky the pharmacy assistant next to me is. Because there is usually more than one pharmacy assistant working per shift, each assistant can focus on one task at a time and interruptions are distributed between them. Together, they can process and prepare a high number of prescriptions and get through their workload efficiently. But the bottleneck will always be at the pharmacist's station, because there is only one pharmacist in most cases and because it takes more time to check prescriptions than to prepare them. The pharmacist risks losing their license if they don't check prescriptions properly. A pharmacy assistant can make a mistake and get away with it because the onus is on the pharmacist to catch those mistakes before they reach the patient. No matter how quickly and efficiently pharmacy assistants complete their tasks, there is usually a backlog of prescriptions waiting by the pharmacist.

Why the problem matters

Limited time prevents pharmacists from achieving the level of service they want to offer. Most pharmacists are attentive to detail and hard-working. They want to do their job properly. They want to spend more time counselling and interacting with their patients. They want to make sure that medical errors and incorrect prescriptions never reach their patients. Surely, lack of time to do so will negatively impact their job satisfaction and mental health in the workplace and worse, will inevitably cause those errors to happen. Patients also want to have more time to ask questions. I felt this numerous times in my practice, whenever a patient had more questions or was anxious to start a medication and needed some additional support. I felt guilty rushing them and anxious myself because I knew I had a pile of prescriptions waiting to be checked. When we don't spend enough time researching medications and talking to our patients, we miss a lot of important details that are essential to providing effective clinical services. We also can't practice to our full scope and our clinical knowledge cannot be consistently applied to help our patients. Lack of time is a huge barrier to the pharmacist adopting a more clinical role and achieving optimal job satisfaction.

Not surprisingly, the amount of medical errors increases when the time spent checking prescriptions decreases. Time constraints in the pharmacy cause medication-related incidents and errors that harm patients. Every year in the United States, 7000 to 9000 people die as a result of a medication error (Tariq et al. 2023). The final opportunity a pharmacist has to check the prescription is at counselling, which almost always happens at the end of the pharmacy workflow. However, when there is a time crunch in the pharmacy, pharmacists may not have the opportunity to counsel their patients or to do so properly. One study on retail pharmacists in the Houston, Texas metropolitan area found that proper counselling by the pharmacist using the designated counselling window was used in only 4 (or 2.6%) of the 153 interactions observed (Yande et al. 2020). This affects the safety and well-being of patients.

Lack of time is an issue not only in the pharmacy profession but in healthcare overall. One medical student writes: "Studies show that during short appointments, physicians are less likely to adhere to published guidelines on medical management and more likely to prescribe additional medications, some of which may not be necessary. There are often other effective interventions prior to starting a medication that the patient may have to take for the rest of their life, yet those solutions inevitably require time to explore" (Hanna 2019). If lack of time is preventing physicians from considering better interventions for their patients, and pharmacists from thoroughly checking what is prescribed by physicians, then we can't guarantee that patients are receiving the best care possible. We are constantly checking prescriptions to be *added* to the patient's profile and we don't have time to think of other options to discuss with the patient and prescriber, such as discontinuing medications or counselling on exercise and diet modifications. As health professionals who swore an oath to protect patients, we should strive to offer interventions that are in patients' best interests. More medications often cause more interactions and unwanted side effects that can worsen patients' health. There are safer options for our patients but a lack of time prevents us from considering them. Retail pharmacists should have enough time to think through all possible drug-related issues whenever they see a new prescription.

The Practical Solutions

To recap, the lack of time in retail pharmacy is due to several issues including:

1. A high volume of prescriptions

2. Having one staff pharmacist on duty in most cases

3. Dealing with interruptions and tasks other than prescription checking.

There isn't really a practical solution to issue number 1. At the end of the day, retail pharmacy is a business and like any other business, it can't turn customers or patients away. Businesses need to make money and it makes sense that businesses offering the best customer service get more customers. Having said that, increasing pharmacist time and allowing them to think critically about new prescriptions will likely reduce the volume of prescriptions. As aforementioned, many patients take drugs that have been prescribed without a clear indication. If pharmacists have enough time to consider which drugs can be replaced by non-medication alternatives, this will not only improve health outcomes for patients but also reduce the pharmacy's workload.

For issue number 2, the obvious solution would be to have more than one pharmacist on duty at a time. This solution is not practical for pharmacies that are not financially capable of employing two or more pharmacists per shift. We will discuss this as an ideal solution in Part 3 of the book. Interruptions (issue number 3) can be managed and they will be discussed in the next chapter.

What can be done if we can't control prescription numbers and it can cost too much to increase staffing levels? It's all about organizing the workload. Prescriptions can be checked in an efficient way that indirectly increases pharmacist time.

A practical solution is to have the entire roster of patients belonging to a specific pharmacy divided into several groups. Refill prescriptions are synchronized for each patient and all refills for each group of patients are checked once every three months by a specific pharmacist. Most chronic medications are refilled every 3 months as this is the maximum most insurance plans will cover at each fill.

Even with limited time to check prescriptions, pharmacists would be checking the prescriptions of the same patients every 3 months, so with time, they would familiarize themselves with patients' medical histories and drug-related issues. The pharmacy would also have fewer interruptions and customer visits because patients would pick up all their pre-scriptions on one day in the given three-month peri-od, rather than on several different days. Of course, there will still be new patients and new prescriptions. Each new patient can be assigned to a specific group under one pharmacist. New prescriptions do not comprise the majority of most pharmacies' work-loads. Refills are usually the cause of lack of time and pharmacy interruptions. Organizing when refills happen and dedicating specific pharmacists to certain groups will make operations more streamlined and efficient, and the pharmacy team better able to handle new prescriptions. There would no longer be prescription checks for patients who were already reviewed that week or earlier in the same day but forgot to pick up another medication. This solution would not reduce the overall number of prescriptions a pharmacist checks each shift, but it would organize the prescriptions in a way that the pharmacist can assess them more easily and efficiently which would help manage their limited time. A general breakdown of how pharmacies can adopt this solution is as follows:

Step 1) This first step will likely take several months to complete. It will require staff to work overtime or during hours when the pharmacy is not open. It is highly recommended to involve pharmacy assistants and technicians wherever possible.

The pharmacy team identifies patients who are on more than one chronic medication, and who fill each of these medications at different times (i.e. not synchronized). Once consent is obtained from these patients, their medication refill quantities should be smaller at each subsequent fill to move refill dates closer together so that all medications can eventually be filled on the same day every three months. The team can enter notes in patient profiles that indicate the dates of upcoming refills and the quantity to fill for each medication.

Step 2) Pharmacists and pharmacy managers/ owners meet up with a complete list of all patients who regularly use the pharmacy. All patients on more than one chronic medication have their refills synchronized at this point. The patient list is divided into groups based on when they require their refills. Groups can also be divided based on medical conditions (e.g. those with diabetes, those with osteoporosis etc) and this can further increase the efficiency of prescription checking as pharmacists would know what general drug therapy issues to look out for in each group.

Groups should be of approximately equal size and each group should have a designated pharmacist who will check that group's prescriptions when they are processed on their assigned day(s). Since there will be more groups than pharmacists, each pharmacist will have more than one group of patients to cover. For example, in a team of three pharmacists where there are 30 groups (one group reviewed every 3 days in the 90-day period), each pharmacist would have 10 groups to cover.

Step 3) Patients in each group should be made aware that all their chronic prescriptions will be filled only on their assigned day(s) every 3 months. Patients would be encouraged to call the pharmacy and/or visit in person only on their assigned day(s).

In summary, this solution can help pharmacy operations become more organized but it will not fully resolve the issue of lack of time. This is because the issue is multifactorial, and as the reader will under-

stand from the next chapters, requires more than one
solution to fully solve it.

Chapter 2:
Barrier 2: Interruptions

The Problem

Pharmacists interpret prescriptions written by physicians, dispense them for patients and make sure they are appropriately covered by insurance providers, all while supervising other pharmacy staff members. It is therefore no wonder a pharmacist will be interrupted by any one of these parties at any given time during their shift. Interruptions in this book are taken to be issues that suddenly arise that cause a break in a pharmacist's current task or the overall pharmacy workflow. Depending on how busy a shift is, it can be tough for a pharmacist to manage a lot of interruptions and try to bring their focus back on checking prescriptions. Phone calls are always coming in and are part of the rhythm of a day's work. Patients and sometimes physicians or other prescribers, are constantly visiting in person and usually ask to speak to the pharmacist. Angry customers occasionally show up and need a staff member to look into a past prescription that was not dispensed to their satisfaction. Drug representatives pop in at random times to meet the pharmacist and discuss a particular drug or device. In addition, some interruptions are due to technical issues. Problems with pharmacy software, limited stock of some medications, and missing information on a prescription all prevent prescriptions from being processed smoothly and in a timely fashion. Even if an interruption doesn't directly affect the pharmacist on duty, pharmacists manage other staff members and are therefore responsible for knowing about everything that affects the overall workflow. Every shift differs in the type and number of interruptions, but there will be interruptions during every shift. It is simply part of the job. Although any experienced retail pharmacist knows this, it can still feel very frustrating to be interrupted while you are checking prescriptions. Nobody likes to be suddenly interrupted several times a day while they are focused on completing important tasks, especially tasks that protect others. This is why interruptions prevent pharmacists from achieving optimal job satisfaction.

Interruptions are also a significant barrier to clinical performance. According to Pharmacy Times, a retail pharmacist can experience up to 7 interruptions in one hour of work (Desselle 2020). These interruptions require a great deal of communication and cognitive function and can therefore lead to burnout for the pharmacist, not to mention errors which may negatively impact patients (Desselle 2020). As alluded to in the previous chapter, interruptions take up a lot of time in the pharmacy - time that is already limited. According to Sinclair et al., pharmacists and technicians took 27% more time to complete a task when they were interrupted versus when they were not interrupted (Sinclair, Slimm, and Terry, 2012).

Many interruptions can impede the retail pharmacy workflow. Because pharmacists mostly deal with patients and their prescribers, the majority of interruptions involve these two parties. Hence, in this chapter, I will only discuss patient and pre-scriber-related interruptions.

Interruptions from patients

Patients or customers can either request the pharmacist's assistance in person (by visiting the pharmacy) or over the phone. According to one study, phone calls are responsible for 64% of all pharmacy interruptions (Burford et al. 2011). Patients usually encounter a pharmacy assistant or technician first before they can request to speak to the pharmacist. Therefore any technical questions (e.g. how many refills are remaining on a prescription, can the pharmacy refill a certain prescription etc.) are usually dealt with by the assistant or technician. Clinical questions (e.g. what to do in case of missed doses, how to take or administer a medication etc.) get passed on to the pharmacist. These questions may require the pharmacist to do some research using either a drug reference or looking into the patient's profile.

Another kind of patient-related interruption is professional services (such as vaccinations, medication reviews, specialized counselling etc.). Although these sometimes happen on an appointment basis, most pharmacies also must provide these services to 'drop-in' patients. The pharmacist on duty has to stop checking prescriptions and leave the dispensary to deliver these services, as they are typically conducted in a private space next to the dispensary. Clinical services take longer than most interruptions to complete because the patient needs to be questioned on their medical and drug-related history, and the pharmacist must document the interaction. Questions about over-the-counter products are also a time-consuming interruption. Patients should be asked about details of their symptoms (the onset, characteristics, location, factors that make the symptoms better or worse) and medical history (allergies, medications they are currently taking) before the pharmacist can

37

recommend a product. Once a product is recommended, the pharmacist should also explain how to use it properly.

According to one study by Reddy et al., patient-related interruptions accounted for 43% of all interruptions encountered by pharmacists (Reddy et al. 2019). Patients generally have unrestricted access to pharmacists. Pharmacists are often coined 'the most accessible healthcare professionals' for this reason. Unlike other health professionals, there is almost always a pharmacist available in every community or within every neighbourhood. Pharmacies are also usually open for longer hours than most prescriber offices, and unlike other health professionals who see their patients on an appointment basis and therefore may not be available when their office phone rings, pharmacists are always nearby when the phone rings. This is great for patients, but it means many interruptions for pharmacists. Another factor contributing to the problem is the physical layout of most pharmacies (Reddy et al. 2019, Jacobs, Hassell and Johnson

2013). Pharmacy workstations (order entry, filling, checking) are customer-facing so that the pharmacy team can acknowledge any customers who come to the counter. Again, this helps provide good customer service however, it's an interruption and potential distraction when the pharmacist has to look up every time someone approaches the counter.

Interruptions from prescribers

Physicians or other prescribers usually communicate with pharmacists via phone calls or fax messages. Depending on whether the prescriber works near the pharmacy, they may visit in person as well. Issues that are considered urgent and are therefore usually interruptions include but are not limited to:

- Changing a prescription written for a patient (e.g. if the pharmacist suggested an alternative medication and the prescriber agrees)

- Drug information question

- Prescriber phoning in a new prescription (in Ontario, only pharmacists and pharmacy technicians can document verbal prescriptions) (Ontario College of Pharmacists 2022)

Fax messages are usually not urgent because the prescriber is aware the pharmacist won't see their message right away when it arrives. Again, it usually goes to a pharmacy assistant or technician who then enters the information into the system (in case of a new prescription) or shows the message to the pharmacist (if there is a prescription change). Phone calls, however, are more urgent. Whenever a prescriber phones in and the phone call is directed to the pharmacist, the pharmacist prioritizes this call over other tasks as they know the prescriber is also busy and it can be difficult to catch them later if they hang up. Also, the pharmacist usually needs the prescriber's authority to solve a prescription-related issue that the pharmacist themself is not authorized to handle. For example, in Ontario, pharmacists are authorized to change the dosage or formulation of a drug on a prescription, but they cannot change the prescription to a different drug without the approval of the prescriber (Ontario College of Pharmacists 2023). Therefore, any issues where the patient cannot take the prescribed drug must be directed back to the prescriber, who may respond with a new prescription. Because the pharmacist is aware the patient is waiting to take the new prescription (often physically waiting in the pharmacy), and the prescriber may be hard to track down at another time, the pharmacist needs to communicate with the prescriber as soon as he/she is available.

There are scenarios where the prescriber is more in need of the pharmacist. For instance, some prescribers have drug-related questions and want to consult a pharmacist. Unless the pharmacist knows the answer, it may take several minutes to respond to these questions as again, the pharmacist must consult one or more references. If such questions are faxed in, the pharmacist may have the option to deal with them later (e.g. at the end of their shift) as they are not as urgent as questions that are phoned in.

The Practical Solutions

I once volunteered at an outpatient pharmacy in a hospital in Saudi Arabia. The pharmacists never received phone calls from patients. Pharmacists would occasionally contact prescribers working in the hospital about drug-related issues. They saw patients face to face for every encounter- both for refill prescriptions and new prescriptions. Refills could also be processed using an app and the patient would be notified when it was ready for pickup, or they can request delivery to their home. The app could also be used to 'ask the pharmacist' any questions. It was a good system because patients who arrived at the pharmacy immediately took a number and waited in the waiting area for their turn. As a large teaching hospital with thousands of patients, there were at least 10 pharmacists on duty at the same time, so of course this made the workflow efficient. Once a patient's number appeared on the screen they came to the appropriate counter, and the pharmacist would be completely focused on that patient with little or no interruptions. There would be no other patients popping up at the counter, no phone calls to deal with (except occasionally to and from prescribers) and, because the pharmacy didn't sell over-the-counter products, no OTC questions. Any prescriptions the patient had would be processed on the spot by the pharmacist, who would then hand over the orders to an assistant or technician working exclusively with that pharmacist, to prepare the medication while the pharmacist counselled the patient or answered any patient questions.

Though some elements of this hospital approach are impractical for a retail setting (i.e. 10 pharmacists each with their own set of pharmacy technicians/ assistants, no over-the-counter products), taking a number may be a practical solution. To pre-

43

vent patients from lingering near the pharmacy counter (a huge distraction for the pharmacy team), patients who want to speak directly to the pharmacist can take a number from one till, and patients who want to process a prescription and would therefore need to see an assistant or technician can take a number from a different till. The order entry assistant/technician on duty and the pharmacist can then ring the numbers up one at a time whenever they finish their current tasks. This will give pharmacists and staff control over situations where there are many customers lined up at the counter. For a business setting, it is unpleasant to see long lines of waiting customers and it also puts more pressure on the pharmacy team to work faster. By taking numbers, patients are indirectly being told it is not their turn now and they can come back soon when it is their turn. Patients' time is also respected in this way as they can feel free to leave the pharmacy or do other tasks (e.g. grab a coffee or make phone calls) if their number is far from being called up.

Some retail pharmacies have buzzers that alert patients when their prescriptions are ready but, in my experience, many patients doubt their buzzer is functioning properly and will come to the counter again if they feel they have waited for too long. Numbers changing on a screen will provide a visual confirmation that there are no technical problems and it will also show them where they are in the line.

Patients who have over-the-counter (OTC) questions can be asked to fill out a form with questions on their symptoms and medical history and to submit this while they are waiting. Patients should be told that in order to see the pharmacist about an OTC question, they must fill out the form. The pharmacist can then review their answers and come up with an appropriate clinical intervention *before* speaking to the patient. This reduces the time it takes for these interactions to occur, as the pharmacist doesn't have to have a full conversation with the patient and do their assessment with the patient standing in front of them. Instead, they can focus on explaining the selected treatment when they see the patient. The patient will also be kept busy while they are waiting, lessening the chance of them interrupting at the pharmacy counter. Note there are cases where the pharmacist must directly see the patient to complete their assessment (e.g. if the patient has a skin condition that the pharmacist must see to assess).

In terms of patient phone call interruptions, the majority are related to refills. Although many retail pharmacies have online or app refill programs, patients who encounter an issue using these programs (e.g. billing problem or less than the full quantity remaining on file), will usually end up calling the pharmacy. Elderly patients may also prefer phoning in their refill requests as they may have difficulty using technology. There are also many calls from patients who have not yet tried these online systems. This can be time-consuming as several of these requests occur every day in most pharmacies. The solution to this is two-fold: 1- the pharmacy needs to ensure their online programs are very user-friendly (especially for elderly patients) and easily accessible, with overrides built in for common technical issues; and 2- the pharmacy team should encourage the use of these programs as often as possible. Patients calling with refill requests can be asked whether they are aware of the pharmacy's online refill program, if available, and *whether they have tried it first before phoning the pharmacy*. It is important to directly ask patients if they have tried it before calling the pharmacy. If staff consistently ask this, patients will feel pressured to try the program first before calling.

For clinical questions, if the pharmacist is busy and cannot answer these questions immediately, the patient's number and information can be written down and the pharmacist can return their call later. I do this sometimes in my current practice. Pharmacists need to know that they shouldn't feel pressured to deal with interruptions immediately when they present. If busy, it is better to focus on current tasks and return to other, less pressing issues afterwards.

Going back to the solution discussed in the previous chapter of organizing the patient roster, if the pharmacy is successful in achieving this, patients can have their prescriptions filled on their specific day. This will eliminate phone calls for refill requests as patients know the pharmacist will review and fill their medications when they run out (usually every three months). Even clinical questions would be called into the patient's specific pharmacist rather than randomly to a pharmacist who may not be familiar with the patient's medication history.

New prescriptions via phone are not common interruptions, however, they can be reduced by encouraging physicians to fax prescriptions to the pharmacy. This will reduce errors and is more legally appropriate as some controlled drugs cannot be verbally prescribed (Ontario College of Pharmacists 2022).

Professional services should be offered on an appointment basis only so that the pharmacist can anticipate when patients will come in and try to prepare for the appointment in advance. The way that these services are reimbursed in Ontario also assumes that the patient and pharmacist met via appointment and not as a drop-in. Immunizations can be offered on only one specific day during the week when the pharmacy may be less busy. The pharmacy can take the names of patients interested in coming in for an immunization that week to prepare consent forms ahead of time and ensure there is an adequate supply of vaccine available.

These are some of the practical solutions pharmacies can implement to help reduce certain common interruptions. Ideally, there would be no interruptions and pharmacists can fully focus on one task at a time. This would involve workflow and business model changes. I will discuss ideal solutions to pharmacy interruptions in the book's final chapter.

50

Chapter 3:

Barrier 3: Lack of pharmacist backup & support

The Problem

I was working the opening shift one morning at a pharmacy when I got a call from my younger sister telling me she had been in a car accident with a semi-truck. Luckily, she was okay but understandably in shock, and she couldn't reach out to anyone else at the time. My first instinct was that I had to leave work and go to support my sister. But when I realized that wouldn't be possible, I got a sick feeling in the pit of my stomach. We had just opened and I was the only pharmacist on duty. If I called my supervisor or another colleague to let them know I had an emergency, it would have taken at least half an hour, in the best of circumstances, for anyone to come in and take over my shift. I couldn't just leave the pharmacy the same way someone can leave their office for an urgent situation. I felt stuck. More importantly, I felt it was wrong that I couldn't leave work for a personal emergency. I wasn't even sure if the pharmacy had a procedure to shut down if I, or any pharmacist on duty, had to physically leave the pharmacy.

The cause of the problem

There are several reasons why retail pharmacists can't leave the pharmacy for a personal emergency or take breaks. In Ontario, a pharmacy can only legally operate if there is a pharmacist physically present (Ontario College of Pharmacists 2024). In other words, no one can have access to any medications contained in a pharmacy (including most over-the-counter medications) if a pharmacist is not on the premises. If a pharmacist has to leave for whatever reason, the pharmacy must be able to implement a 'lock and leave', where the entire pharmacy closes or barriers must be put up around areas where there are medications to prevent access to the public (Ontario College of Pharmacists 2024).

Another factor contributing to the issue is that in Ontario, pharmacists are not protected by employment laws. The Employment Standards Act or ESA is an Ontario law that states that no employee shall work for more than 5 consecutive hours without at least a 30-minute break (Ministry of Labour, Immigration, Training and Skills Development 2023). However, there is a special exemptions section for this law for health professionals, including pharmacists (Ministry of Labour, Immigration, Training and Skills Development 2022). It states that pharmacists and pharmacy students are not entitled to:

- Minimum wage

- Daily and weekly limits on hours of work

- Daily rest periods

- Time off between shifts

- Weekly/ bi-weekly rest periods

- Eating periods

- Overtime pay

- Sick leave, family responsibility leave or bereavement leave if taking the leave would be professional misconduct or abandoning your duty

- Public holidays or public holiday pay

- Vacation with pay

The first time I read this list I couldn't believe it. Pharmacists not being allowed to take breaks or emergency leaves was always an unwritten rule to me. I didn't realize we were excluded from a law protecting all employees in Ontario. In fact, whenever I started a new pharmacy position I was given a one-sheet summary of ESA employee rights. This sheet never included the exemptions applicable to pharmacists. What's the point in giving pharmacists this sheet if the employee rights listed on it don't apply to our profession?

Recently there has been a lot of focus on expanding pharmacists' scope of practice in Ontario. But pharmacy stakeholders working with the government should focus on addressing this crazy ESA exemptions list first. What good is an expanded scope if we can't ensure that pharmacists are working in an environment that supports their mental and physical well-being?

The exemptions list was created because health professionals have a duty to respond to patient needs (Ministry of Labour 2017). However, if the health professional is thinking about the accident that just happened to their loved one, or about how they feel nauseous and want to vomit but have to keep going because they can't leave work, what good are their services to those patients?

In 2017, the Ontario government asked for input about the ESA exemptions from pharmacists (Ontario College of Pharmacists 2017). But since then I haven't seen any changes to retail pharmacist working conditions.

Furthermore, the exemptions impact community pharmacists more than other health professionals and hospital pharmacists. Community pharmacists are easy to access and work in stores visited by customers who can come in almost any hour of the day or night. A retail pharmacy is not appointment-based like an office that opens at 8 am and closes at 4 pm with a lunch break from 12 to 1 pm. Also, there is typically only one pharmacist on duty per shift unlike in hospitals where there are usually several pharmacists available on site if one takes a break. Retail pharmacies are businesses that must be profitable so if only one pharmacist is enough to check the number of prescriptions the pharmacy receives, there will be only one pharmacist on duty. On the other hand, the types of patients a community pharmacist sees differ from those in the care of a hospital pharmacist. Although I agree with the ESA that a pharmacist shouldn't be absent at a time when a patient requiring urgent care is present, community pharmacy patients are, in the vast majority of cases, ambulatory and not acutely ill. A well-deserved break for a community pharmacist would very likely not kill anyone or significantly delay their treatment - they are being treated in a non-acute, outpatient community setting after all.

If the law doesn't protect pharmacists, large pharmacy corporations will take advantage of this to make more profits. Pharmacy companies focus on putting customers first, even when it comes to the basic needs of pharmacists. Customers bring in profits and pharmacists are part of the business expense. This business culture creates the customer expectation that there will always be a pharmacist available. I remember once working as a student when the pharmacist on duty had to hide in the back room to quickly grab her lunch. She soon had to come back out of the room to help a customer while she was still munching on her food. She couldn't sit down and have a peaceful break for 10 minutes before being needed in the dispensary again. It wasn't an urgent issue the patient needed her for - it was something that could have waited until she finished her lunch. However, retail pharmacy patients are used to seeing a pharmacist in front of them whenever they need one. They are also used to pharmacies competing to provide the best customer service. How a business operates and 'trains' its customers, and how competitor businesses operate, greatly impact customer expectations.

Why the problem matters

It's not hard to see how serious the consequences of this issue can be. Pharmacists are responsible for providing patient care and preventing harm from reaching patients. If they are not well rested and nourished, there will be errors and inefficiencies - plain and simple. Of course, there will inevitably always be errors because pharmacists are humans, at the end of the day. But a fatigued human will make more errors than a non-fatigued human. Although I was unable to find data for pharmacists, one source indicates that 65% of tired nurses make medication errors (McKeen & Associates, P.C. 2021).

Lack of adequate breaks can also cause mental health problems and burnout for pharmacists. One study in French community pharmacies found that work-related stress was significantly associated with fatigue, sleep disturbances, anxiety and depression (Balayssac et al. 2017). Several factors associated with stress were identified in the study, including demanding patients, too many patients, feeling overwhelmed and not supported, fear of dispensing incorrect medications, dissatisfaction with the work atmosphere and deterioration of work quality (Balayssac et al. 2017). Having regular scheduled breaks, a supportive environment and more work-life balance would undoubtedly improve pharmacists' job satisfaction, efficiency and ultimately, pharmacy profits.

What we are currently seeing in the retail pharmacist job market is high burnout and quitting rates (Peebles 2022). With increased pressure from the coronavirus pandemic of 2019, the profession lost several qualified pharmacists and pharmacy technicians due to burnout. According to a Bloomberg article, two of the largest pharmacy chains in the U.S. - Walgreens and CVS- have had unfilled positions for months throughout the pandemic and both were offering sign-on bonuses (Peebles 2022). Another article states that CVS closed 900 stores due to staffing shortages, and the following year, announced they would provide their (remaining) staff with a dedicated, uninterrupted daily lunch break in which their pharmacies would close for 30 minutes and customers would be aware of the daily closure (Levy 2022). It would be interesting to see how this mandatory break will impact business, and hopefully, chain pharmacies in Canada and around the world can adopt a similar policy soon. We shouldn't have to wait for pharmacists and pharmacy staff to quit to make these changes that will obviously have positive impacts on staff, customers and businesses overall.

The Practical Solutions

In the remainder of this chapter, we will discuss a couple of practical solutions that would allow pharmacists to take regular breaks during their shifts and have coverage for emergencies. The solutions here will not involve changing the laws and current policies governing pharmacy because they are meant to be solutions that pharmacy owners, managers and pharmacists can implement right away. Ideal solutions will be discussed later in the book.

How to provide pharmacists with breaks

The main concept to keep in mind here is that once a pharmacist leaves the pharmacy, the pharmacy cannot operate in the same way. Drugs cannot be dispensed or be accessible for sale to patients, and orders cannot be completed because they require a pharmacist's clinical check. So pharmacies with only one pharmacist on duty per shift have two options here: either perform a lock and leave, or the pharmacist can take a break but still be present in the pharmacy. The pharmacist shouldn't be taking their break where drugs are dispensed but rather in a private space (e.g. counselling room, storage room, office) within the pharmacy. In this way, the pharmacy can still technically operate without performing a lock and leave. Staff members and patients should be informed of this daily break period (of which there can be two if pharmacists work both morning and evening shifts at the pharmacy) and should be asked to respect the pharmacist's time off unless there is an emergency. Pharmacists should always take their breaks (even if they feel they don't need one) and try to be consistent with the timing of breaks so that customers know what to expect. Most importantly, the pharmacist should not be interrupted during their break.

The following are common interruptions and how they can be handled while the pharmacist is on break:

1- A patient has a question, requires counselling or a professional service

Patients can be consistently informed that the pharmacist on duty takes a daily break from 12:30 to 1 pm (for example) and will not be available during this time. If patients are consistently told this, they will be trained to not expect the pharmacist during this time and to come in at a different time if they would like to see the pharmacist. Nearby pharmacies can also work together to have overlapping break times. That way, patients turned away during the break time of Pharmacist A at Pharmacy A can go to nearby Pharmacy B where Pharmacist B will not yet be on break. Likewise, when Pharmacist B is on break, patients with urgent drug questions can come to Pharmacist A. In rural settings where there are not many pharmacies, staff may refer patients with urgent questions to call pharmacies elsewhere. Even if the patient's question is related to the medications they take, in an urgent situation any pharmacist can help them or will know where to find the answer. Staff members can help make the call to another pharmacy to provide information on the medications the patient takes if necessary. Alternatively, if the question is related to a specific medication, many drug companies have patient drug information phone numbers that can be found online or on the medication packaging.

For patients requiring counselling on new prescriptions, the pharmacist can call them before or after their break or even at the end of their shift. Methadone clinics, immunization appointments and medication reviews should not be scheduled during a pharmacist's break time.

2- There is a phone call for the pharmacist from a patient or prescriber

Patients and prescribers calling to speak to the pharmacist can either call back at a later time, or the pharmacist can call them back. However, staff should not always promise that the pharmacist will call back as this may create long lists of people the pharmacist has to call after their break, and this can be overwhelming. It is important to avoid backlogging work as much as possible so that when the pharmacist returns from their break, the workflow will continue to be smooth. If the prescriber is calling a new prescription in, the staff team can ask if it can be faxed instead.

3- There are urgent orders (sometimes referred to as 'reds') to be checked

These orders are usually urgent because patients would like to wait in the pharmacy for them. They are also typically new prescriptions (e.g. antibiotics) rather than refills of medications they have taken before. When new prescriptions are dropped off, the staff team usually gives the patient a wait time to let them know when the prescription will be ready. Wait times have to be adjusted to account for the pharmacist's break. If the pharmacy is really busy, they can offer to deliver the patient's medication and provide phone counselling later. Again, part of the issue is that customers expect fast service and a pharmacist that is always available. Retail pharmacy customers solemnly present with life-threatening conditions that require very urgent care. If customers are trained that the pharmacist takes a daily break at a specific time(s) and that the wait time for prescriptions around this break time is much longer than at other times in the day, they will change their expectations. Patients always have the choice of which pharmacy to dispense their medications at, so if they cannot wait for long, they can go to another pharmacy. Of course, pharmacy owners and executives reading this may not like it. The ideal situation would be that all pharmacies give their pharmacists a 30-minute break, so there won't be competition between pharmacies for business. In other words, no matter which pharmacy they go to, customers have to expect a longer wait time at some point during the day for breaks. But this will only happen if laws change (more on this later in the book).

4- A drug representative or other staff member would like to speak to the pharmacist about a work-related issue

Drug representatives and visitors should be informed that the pharmacist is on break and they can follow up at a later time. Staff members should only interrupt the pharmacist during break time if there is an emergency or urgent issue (e.g. a technical problem that requires the pharmacist's password, the pharmacist is required for an intervention in order for the rest of the staff team to carry on with their duties, or a patient presents with a severe condition). Staff may have to be trained in recognizing severe medical conditions (e.g. anaphylaxis, asthma attack) and it may be reasonable to have at least one other full-time staff member trained in CPR and First Aid. Other technical problems can be resolved by calling the pharmacy's software/ hardware provider.

Minimizing interruptions will ensure the pharmacist can take maximum advantage of their time off to clear their mind and refresh themselves. Interruptions are constantly happening in a pharmacy as previously discussed, so pharmacists deserve and should be allowed a period of zero interruptions during their shift the same way other staff are. It is bad enough that the pharmacist cannot leave the pharmacy building to take a break outside of work - they should at least have a peaceful break. The pharmacist will likely return to a large pile of prescriptions to be checked, so the staff team should try, as much as possible, to minimize other tasks required of the pharmacist when they return (i.e. callbacks to patients and prescribers).

The advantages of having a formal store-wide lock and leave as in CVS pharmacies across the US is that there will be no business operations during this time and all staff, including pharmacists, can take their break wherever they want (inside or outside the pharmacy). There would be no interruptions and customers again would become 'trained' to know that the pharmacy closes at the same time each day for breaks - the same way their doctor's office might close midday for the same reason. The only disadvantage of this method is that it would require the intervention of head management for most pharmacies with a corporate structure, so it may take longer to implement. However, it would be easier to implement for independent pharmacies with a sole owner.

How to ensure backup coverage for emergencies

Life happens and there will be times when a pharmacist can't make it to a shift and last-minute changes to the work schedule have to be made. These times can be very stressful for everyone, including those who are called upon to cover last minute. Similar to how on-call schedules are made in hospitals and other healthcare settings, retail pharmacies can have a backup on-call schedule for these situations. The on-call person will be on stand-by, aware that they might be called in to cover. If they are called, they shouldn't be unavailable as they agreed to be on-call for that day or for the specific time period.

Although it would take more time and effort to create, the on-call schedule can be made whenever the work schedule (for the upcoming month or two, for example) is created. The staff member responsible for making the schedule should ask for availability not only for the main shifts to be covered but also for backup shifts. Each shift would therefore have the main pharmacist who is expected to show up and a backup pharmacist who would cover *only in exceptional circumstances*. It should be made clear to the pharmacist team that this backup schedule is not to be abused, and that anticipated time off for personal reasons (e.g. vacations, appointments etc.) should be booked before the creation of the schedule. Backups should only be called upon in unforeseen emergency situations.

The backup schedule will work well in pharmacy teams where there are many pharmacists. Each individual would be on-call only a few times a month in a large team. Smaller pharmacist teams (e.g. those belonging to independent pharmacies) can choose not to have an on-call schedule and instead perform a lock and leave whenever there is an emergency involving the on-duty pharmacist. Patients can be made aware with a sign on the pharmacy door saying that the pharmacy had to close early due to an emergency. Other staff members could stay back once the pharmacy closes its doors to make phone calls to patients expected to come in that day, to ask if they would like their medications delivered or if they can pick up the following day. Urgent prescriptions that haven't been processed yet could be transferred to other pharmacies. Smaller independent pharmacies generally provide more one-on-one services to their clientele and have strong relationships with customers. They will therefore gain their respect and understanding, in most cases, in these situations. Alternatively, the pharmacy can have a list of several backup relief pharmacists (e.g. other pharmacist colleagues or friends of the pharmacy owner) that could be called to come in for emergency coverage.

One disadvantage of the on-call schedule is that it still won't ensure *immediate* coverage in emergencies. If the on-call pharmacist lives too far away, it may take a while before they arrive at the pharmacy. Some emergencies can't wait. Thus, pharmacy owners should train staff on how to perform a lock and leave in these situations, until the on-call pharmacist arrives.

In summary, there are simple solutions that can be implemented without policy and law changes to help pharmacists have more fulfilling jobs and provide better work-life balance. Pharmacy companies and owners should not be afraid of losing customers at the expense of their pharmacists' health and well-being. As long as break times are communicated clearly and consistently to customers, they will adapt to them. If the service they are provided at the pharmacy is maintained or improved, which it very likely will be if their pharmacist has a daily break, pharmacies won't lose customers for implementing break periods. Likewise, emergencies don't happen every day, so the majority of clients won't be upset if their pharmacy has to close temporarily and it is communicated to them. Ultimately, all pharmacies should be legally required to provide breaks and implement the lock and leave policy when required. If there is no legal requirement, pharmacies will continue competing with each other to process as many prescriptions

and provide as many services as possible during their
opening hours.

Chapter 4:

Barrier 4: Limited patient information

The Problem

Retail pharmacists often don't have as many details as they should about a patient's medical history, and even their complete medication history. The knowledge we have about our patients should not be limited to their address, date of birth, whether they have insurance and a list of the medications they have filled at our pharmacy. Our pharmacy dispensing software focuses on these aspects of our patients. But if we want to adopt a more clinical role and more fulfilling career moving forward, we need to know things like whether a patient's lab values warrant stopping a certain medication, whether a medication is actually improving a patient's medical condition or is just being refilled blindly every 3 months, and whether a patient is taking their medication correctly. We can only know this information if we communicate with our patients and their other health providers, and if we have access to our patients' medical records.

The problem in this chapter can be described as a lack of communication - between patients and their pharmacists, between pharmacies, and between other healthcare providers and retail pharmacists. There is no doubt that this is a major barrier to the retail pharmacist's ability to provide clinically-focused care.

The cause of the problem

One of the main reasons why pharmacists have very limited and usually non-clinical data for their patients is the lack of time to gather this important information. To be accurate, clinical information must be collected from multiple sources including a patient interview, medical reports and data provided by the patient's prescribers and other pharmacies if applicable. Gathering this kind of data, inputting it into pharmacy software and interpreting it every time a medication is dispensed for a patient would take a considerable amount of time that a busy retail pharmacist simply doesn't have. The current business model therefore also plays a role in this issue. With the focus being on dispensing medications to make profits, pharmacists are pressured to work fast rather than to take their time to think through each encounter as a clinical case. The pharmacy business model must shift from being focused on selling medications to treating patients. It must allow enough time to gather the appropriate information from patients, other health providers and other resources such as the Clinical Viewers now available to community pharmacies in Ontario.

Another factor contributing to the problem is that patients are not used to giving this information to their pharmacist. I have completed medication reviews with patients who have questioned why I need the information about their medical conditions, or who have hesitated to offer this information. Some patients see a retail pharmacy as a place to pay for and pick up their medications, not a place where they should be asked about their health information. At the same time, we pharmacists have to change our perceptions of patients and treat them as *our patients* rather than just customers. Our unique position as healthcare providers and medication vendors can make it hard to remember this. I have even been using the terms customers and patients interchangeably thus far throughout the book. They are patients first and customers second.

Why the problem matters

Pharmacies today are offering more clinical services to patients than ever before. Pharmacists are starting to adopt clinical roles and moving away from technical duties in the pharmacy. Having enough information about our patients and their medical conditions allows our clinical services to be meaningful. It ensures that they will be effective and not cause any harm to our patients. Without detailed patient information, there will be room for medication errors and reduced quality of care.

The information we currently have in our systems is not comprehensive enough. For example, certain medications and allergens may be listed under a patient's allergies in their profile, but without details on the specific reactions and when they occurred. In addition, pharmacy systems always flag drug interactions, but usually without details on the patient's weight, kidney function, liver function and other lab values. Thus the pharmacist is not always able to interpret allergies and interactions to determine whether they are significant or not. When there are many flags, it is easier for pharmacists to ignore them - a phenomenon called alert fatigue (Alert Fatigue 2019). Pharmacists are constantly being alerted to interactions or drug issues that cannot be fully assessed, so they choose the less time-consuming solution of ignoring them. After all, these alerts occur mostly for refills of medications the patient already takes. If they haven't had any issues with the medication thus far, it is easier and quicker to assume they won't have any future issues. This approach can be harmful and the patient could be at risk for negative health outcomes. However, if a pharmacist has enough time and the right information available, they will be able to fully assess potential drug problems, rather than just assuming there won't be any.

Detailed patient information doesn't just improve our role as clinicians, and the health and safety of our patients. It also improves business. When we gather and use clinical information at each patient encounter, we build trust and better relationships with our patients. This can yield better customer retention and higher revenues.

The Practical Solutions

As aforementioned, this issue is multifactorial and the best solution is one that would involve changing the current business model that retail pharmacies operate under. That would be an ideal solution. In this section, however, we will discuss a couple of practical solutions.

The most obvious solution for Ontario pharmacies is to start registering for and using the eHealth Ontario Clinical Viewer. Even with limited time in the pharmacy, having this tool available and using it whenever possible will help pharmacists become more familiar with it. As pharmacists familiarize themselves with the tool, they will become more efficient at gathering information from it. This tool is a step in the right direction for the government and pharmacy stakeholders as they recognize that pharmacists are clinicians. By registering for it, pharmacists are acknowledging the need for this resource.

Another solution for all pharmacies (including those that don't have a tool like the Clinical Viewer available in their region) is to provide patients with clinical information forms that they can fill out either alone or, preferably, with their family doctors or primary prescribers. These forms can ask for a list of medical conditions and family medical history, detailed information on allergies, over-the-counter medications the patient uses (e.g. vitamins, minerals, herbal remedies) and their indications, and social history (e.g. occupation, details on diet and exercise, smoking). Patients can fill out these forms on their own time and return them to the pharmacy team to update their files. To avoid concern among patients as to why this information is being gathered, pharmacy staff can alert patients picking up their medications that the pharmacy is in the process of gathering detailed clinical information so that pharmacists can provide better care. If patients know ahead of time what to expect and why, they are more likely to cooperate.

These forms will also show patients' physicians that pharmacists want to be included in the circle of care. The blame for the lack of communication with health providers goes both ways - other professionals are also busy and we can't assume it is their responsibility to communicate with us pharmacists. We can take the initiative and show interest and this will encourage more interprofessional collaboration.

Gradually updating files with information from these forms can be done during slow periods, or the pharmacy owner/ manager may consider having a staff member come in for a couple of hours each week. Having this information in the patient's profile will save precious pharmacist time during medication reviews and other clinical services.

Clinical services provide another great opportunity for pharmacists to gather and update patient information. For example, many pharmacies offer flu vaccines during dedicated clinic times (with an additional pharmacist) throughout the busy flu season. Administering a vaccine takes less than 5 minutes in most cases. Pharmacy owners/ managers can therefore consider creating 10-minute or 15-minute slots to allow pharmacists time to interview patients and update their medical information.

With these solutions, patients, pharmacists and other health providers will start embracing the pharmacist's clinical role. However, if the business model doesn't change, there is only so much a pharmacist can do with the information they gather and input into patient profiles. Pharmacists will still need more time and a shift of focus from selling to treating, to thoroughly assess and document clinical information at every patient encounter.

Chapter 5 :
Barrier 5: Current business model

The current retail pharmacy business model is focused on dispensing and selling more and more medications rather than providing care that benefits patients and maximizes the use of pharmacists' clinical skills. In this chapter, we will discuss how the current retail pharmacy business model is a barrier to pharmacists' job satisfaction and their ability to adopt a more clinical role. In my opinion, most solutions to the business model problem are complex and involve legislative changes. Potential legislative changes will also be discussed in this chapter.

The Problem

It is important to define what I mean by 'retail pharmacy business model.' It is the way that pharmacies operate and serve patients. There are three sub-problems I would like to address in this chapter:

workflow inefficiencies, patient expectations and selling as the main focus. You will find there is a lot of overlap between business model issues and the barriers discussed in the previous chapters.

Workflow Inefficiencies

Although there may be several inefficiencies in the pharmacy workflow, we will discuss three common ones in this section: the pharmacist's physical position in the workflow, how prescriptions enter the pharmacy and the intermittent provision of clinical services in a busy retail setting.

Inefficiency #1: Physical position of the pharmacist

In many pharmacies, the pharmacist checks prescriptions after they have been dispensed by other staff members. The pharmacist doesn't even see the prescription from the doctor until it has been entered into the system, processed, and the medication fully prepared and labelled. This means that if the pharmacist identifies an issue with the prescription or the patient's ability to take the drug (e.g. incorrect dose, allergy, interaction, lower-cost alternative), the entire order would have to be cancelled and the medication returned to the beginning of the workflow to be re-processed and labelled. Valuable pharmacy time will be wasted cancelling orders whose issues could have been addressed right at the start. In addition, when the pharmacist is at the end of the workflow line completing the final check, this check will be more technical than clinical (when there is no pharmacy technician available). In other words, the pharmacist will focus on checking details such as correct la-belling, correct amount dispensed, expiry dates and so on rather than whether the drug is appropriate for the patient or not. When there is no dispensed prod-uct to check (i.e. at the beginning of the workflow line), the pharmacist will be fully focused on the clin-ical details.

Furthermore, the pharmacist's position at the end of the line shows patients that their prescription is almost ready but the 'pharmacist just has to check it'. It makes it seem like the very important work of clinically checking a prescription is the last small step between patients and their already prepared medication when really it is the most important service any pharmacy has to offer. If the pharmacist wasn't there, the patient would be out the door much faster. But at what cost? Their safety? Their life? Placing the pharmacist at the beginning puts less pressure on the pharmacist to perform the clinical check faster. It also shows patients and the pharmacy staff team that some medications may not have to be processed or shouldn't be processed at all - it depends on the pharmacist's assessment. It indicates to them that there is a clinical check and that is what dictates whether and how they receive their prescription. The main concern should be their safety - not how quickly they can leave the pharmacy.

Inefficiency #2: How prescriptions enter the pharmacy

The second workflow inefficiency I would like to discuss is the way that prescriptions come into a pharmacy. Most pharmacies accept prescriptions via fax, phone or in person. Having multiple ways for a prescription to enter a pharmacy can be very convenient for prescribers and especially for patients. However, it limits the pharmacy team's ability to focus and be efficient with their tasks. Phones always ringing, fax machines that have to be constantly checked, and patients popping up at the counter all reduce the efficiency of the pharmacy workflow as they are major interruptions. This, in turn, reduces the staff team's and pharmacist's job satisfaction. Furthermore, if the pharmacist is going to be placed at the beginning of the workflow line to clinically check prescriptions before they are processed, having multiple prescription entry points will be overwhelming for the pharmacist. If all prescriptions came in via only one route, it would be much easier to prioritize them and stay organized.

I saw this in a hospital pharmacy setting - all the new doctors' orders came in via fax only. Yes, there were a lot of faxes throughout the day, but it was easier to know that you didn't have to deal with phone calls or walk-ins for new prescriptions. Of course, the issue is that if the fax machine breaks down, there are no alternative routes for prescriptions to come into the pharmacy. However, this rarely occurs and usually technical issues like this can be solved on the same day. The other concern is that in a retail setting where the primary focus is to sell, there should be as many options for prescriptions to enter the pharmacy as possible to make it convenient for customers and to maximize opportunities for making profits. My argument here is that efficiency is the greater convenience for customers as it means their prescriptions will be ready sooner. If streamlining all prescriptions to enter via one route means faster, more accurate prescription processing, most patients likely won't mind.

Each route comes with its advantages and disadvantages. For example, if all prescriptions were phoned in, you would have to dedicate one or two staff members to answering the phone the whole day. Keep in mind the laws of taking prescriptions by phone. In Ontario, prescriptions for some controlled drugs cannot be taken by phone, and only a pharmacy technician or pharmacist may take new prescription orders verbally (Ontario College of Pharmacists 2023). It would not be a good use of resources to have a technician or pharmacist on the phone all day, as they also have to check prescriptions. On the other hand, any prescription issues could be dealt with right away with the prescriber. For example, if a physician calls in with a prescription for a medication that is back-ordered, the pharmacist could discuss other options with the prescriber while they are on the phone rather than having to fax them later and wait for a response. Also, if verbal orders are immediately documented electronically, phone-only prescriptions could help create paperless pharmacies with reduced clutter and a smaller environmental impact.

Eliminating all but one prescription entry route is a viable option for retail pharmacies, though I consider it an ideal solution rather than a practical solution that can be easily implemented. It would require legislative change because businesses compete with one another for customer satisfaction. If one pharmacy eliminates all but one route for prescription entry, it may lose customers to other pharmacies. In the book's final chapter, we will discuss how new prescriptions can come in via fax only, and by prescribers only. Patient refill requests via phone and in person can be eliminated if medications are proactively reviewed by pharmacists and prepared before patients need them.

Inefficiency #3: Intermittent provision of clinical services

The third workflow inefficiency I would like to discuss is the provision of clinical services in an intermittent manner in retail pharmacies. Clinical services should be provided at every encounter between a pharmacist and a patient; not just when the pharmacist has a few extra minutes to spare. Pharmacists have a professional duty to provide valuable clinical care to patients. Most retail pharmacies do not have the time or proper physical environments to provide clinical services regularly. They are just seen as a bonus revenue stream, and unfortunately, some pharmacies take shortcuts to provide them. A 2016 study on Medschecks claims in Ontario found that annual Medschecks were less likely to be provided in high-volume pharmacies (Pechlivanoglou 2016). This is not surprising, as pharmacists working in busier pharmacies have less time to complete medication reviews. The more concerning finding in this study, however, was that Medschecks recipients were more likely to be healthy, younger, and on fewer medications (Pechlivanoglou 2016). This means that patients who would benefit most from the Medscheck service (i.e. older patients on several chronic medications), were not receiving them. Due to time and working environment constraints, pharmacies abuse the provision of these services by offering them to easy patients who would take less time to review and earn the same profit as a more complex patient on multiple medications.

Patient expectations

Since pharmacy is a business and patients are the customers, the retail pharmacy business model is more convenient for patients than it is for pharmacists. As mentioned in Part 1 of the book, patients have the right to choose their pharmacies. It is up to the patient to decide based on the level of service they get, and the dispensing fee the pharmacies charge. From a clinical point of view, this does not promote continuity of care for pharmacists. Patients should not be allowed to dispense different medications at separate pharmacies. If they want to transfer out of a pharmacy, they should transfer *all* their medications, not just one or a few (as is currently the case).

Furthermore, patients expect pharmacies to dispense their medications as fast as possible. They don't see the process as being a clinical one. Rather, they believe that all the pharmacy staff has to do is count their pills or pour the medication into a vial, label it and hand it to them. They are usually unaware of potential billing issues, the clinical check and the legal requirements for dispensing drugs. Why is the pharmacist taking forever to give me this drug that the doctor already said was going to work for me? What is the pharmacist doing anyway? I hope that some of the readers of this book are pharmacy patrons and I hope these chapters have shed light on what happens on the other side of the counter. A pharmacist can do so much more for patients than just stick a label on a vial and make sure the amount of medication is correct.

If we want our business model to reflect clinical care, we have to consider what impression we give patients when they walk into a pharmacy. Most of the time they see a pharmacist who is standing in what looks like an assembly line, with their head bowed down, looking very busy. This will give the impression that a pharmacy is like a fast food restaurant, and will have their medications ready within minutes. If instead, they see a pharmacist sitting in an office with clinical references and detailed patient information at their fingertips, who is available by appointment only, their expectations will change. If patients are trained that their medications will not be ready on the same day they are ordered, their expectations will change. Retail pharmacy will be more of a pharmacy providing care and less of a business that's just trying to make money.

Selling as the main focus

It is often recognized that retail pharmacists face a conflict of interest. They are supposed to advise patients regarding the same medications they are selling to them. But for every pharmacist, the oath sworn at the beginning of their career should always take precedence over their job to sell. The important thing is for pharmacy companies to realize this.

As discussed in Chapter 1, we seldom ask ourselves whether a patient should *stop* taking a given medication because of limited time and pressure to maintain profits. For instance, medications like proton pump inhibitors (used to treat heartburn or reflux) are often refilled for too long. These drugs are safe to use for a short period (i.e., 2 to 8 weeks) but when taken chronically can cause low magnesium levels, infections, and can increase osteoporosis risk (Bain et al. 2008). Instead of investigating whether a patient needs a drug, pharmacists face pressure to continue dispensing and checking an endless amount of prescriptions

There is often also pressure to sell professional services. One employee review of a chain retail pharmacy states that pharmacists are called every 3 hours daily to report MedsCheck numbers (Glassdoor 2015). With a reimbursement of $25-150 each, it is no wonder pharmacy corporations see them as attractive revenue opportunities, especially when compared to prescriptions which are usually dispensed with a fee of less than $15 each. However, it is not ethical for clinical pharmacy work to be performed just for the profits. There must be a need for clinical interventions and patients must benefit from them.

The business of pharmacy currently rewards high volumes of dispensed prescriptions and clinical services, rather than the quality of clinical care provided. This is common in healthcare, where quantity is rewarded more than quality. Perhaps this is because it is difficult to measure quality in healthcare. For example, if we reward healthcare outcomes like preventing hospitalizations or strokes, how do we know that a specific pharmacist's intervention is what prevented the stroke from happening? There could be multiple confounding factors contributing to the outcome. There can, however, be financial incentives to encourage better quality of clinical services. Let's say annual medication reviews should take at least 30 minutes per encounter. A pharmacy with a dedicated clinical pharmacist wouldn't be expected to complete more than 15 annual reviews daily, assuming an 8-hour shift and a 30-minute break. Pharmacies that complete an appropriate number of reviews per day (given their staffing and hours of operation) could be reimbursed more money per review than pharmacies completing too many reviews.

The goal can't be to sell - businesses must focus on treating patients and doing so ethically. There must be tougher laws in place to regulate pharmacy companies.

Legislative changes required for the business model problem

Disclaimer: These changes are suggestions only and the author's own opinion.

1) It should be illegal for head office, pharmacy owners and managers to ask their employee pharmacists how many services they have provided or whether they have met specific quotas. The decision to dispense a medication or perform a clinical service and how to perform it should rest entirely with the pharmacist. Decisions should not be made under pressure to satisfy customers and perform faster.

2) It should be a legal requirement for every pharmacy that is financially capable of doing so, to employ at least two pharmacists for every shift. Every pharmacy should have a pharmacist dedicated to providing medication reviews whenever the pharmacy is open.

Pharmacies that are not capable of hiring two pharmacists per shift should at least have a pharmacist and pharmacy technician working every shift. The financial capability of pharmacies could be assessed by business consultants hired by licensing bodies.

3) Pharmacists should legally be allowed at least a 30-minute break per shift. For longer shifts (e.g. 12 hours) pharmacists should be allowed at least two 30-minute breaks. Lock and leaves should be a legal daily requirement of pharmacies employing only one pharmacist per shift, to allow that pharmacist to take a daily break. In emergencies, pharmacists should have the legal right to lock up as soon as they need to (shouldn't be required to wait for a backup pharmacist to show up before locking and leaving the store).

4) It should be a legal requirement that all new prescriptions be faxed directly from prescriber

offices to pharmacies. Prescriptions should not be phoned in, and should not be provided to patients to bring to their pharmacy.

5) Patients should be legally required to have all their prescriptions dispensed at one pharmacy. If a patient chooses to switch pharmacies, *all* of their prescriptions should be transferred to the other pharmacy. In exceptional circumstances (e.g. the patient is out of town and ran out of one medication and needs it refilled at a different pharmacy or the patient urgently needs a medication and their pharmacy is closed), prescriptions should be transferred back to the original pharmacy after they are dispensed. Patients could sign a form to indicate their understanding and agreement with this legal requirement.

In the final chapter, we will look at how an ideal pharmacy (a *Phresh Pharmacy*) can operate assuming all these legislative changes are in place.

Part 3:
The Phresh Pharmacy

' You walk into a Phresh Pharmacy, and what do you see? What do you hear? As a pharmacy customer, you want to see staff members who are approachable and ready to spend as much time as you need to address your concerns. You want to hear the words 'How may I help you?' rather than your throat clearing as you try to get the attention of staff whose heads are bowed down buried in work. As a pharmacist, you want to see just one or two happy patients in front of you rather than lines of frustrated customers. You want to hear your voice counselling those patients and their voices responding and absolutely no phone calls interrupting your conversations. Most importantly, you want to feel comfortable and relaxed at your place of work, not stressed and crunched for time. You and each of your patients want all your attention on the one patient in front of you, rather than being constantly distracted and interrupted.

A Phresh Pharmacy is my vision for an ideal (but not impossible) pharmacy. It represents all the changes - legislative, business-related, and profession-related - that I believe need to happen for retail pharmacists to be satisfied with their jobs and to provide the highest level of clinical care they are capable of providing.

The Vision

In Chapter 1 we discussed a practical solution where patient refills are synchronized and patients are encouraged to visit the pharmacy once every three months to minimize interruptions and increase pharmacist efficiency. Each pharmacist is responsible for a certain number of groups and they oversee the processing of prescriptions for those groups on their respective days. As new patients join the pharmacy, they will get assigned to a group.

In a Phresh Pharmacy, refills are also synchronized and pharmacists are still responsible for their groups of patients so they can familiarize themselves with patient medications and medical histories. However, prescriptions are not just blindly refilled. Medication reviews are completed every three months during appointments between the pharmacist and patient. There will be patients who need to follow up more frequently with their pharmacist (e.g. if they are starting a new therapy that requires clinical monitoring), and those who will require less frequent follow-up (e.g. younger patients on fewer therapies or with no clinical changes). Appointments therefore don't necessarily have to be in person - they can be quick virtual or phone appointments depending on the type of follow-up.

Every pharmacy would be required to have two pharmacists working together per shift - one to cover appointments with their patients and the other to complete clinical checks of new prescriptions. Pharmacies that don't have the financial capability to hire two pharmacists per shift would have one pharmacist and one registered pharmacy technician per shift. Patient appointments would happen in an office space in or near the pharmacy. The dispensary would be for medication preparation and pick-up. Pharmacists would rotate between covering appointments and working in the dispensary. Each pharmacist would also have access to the pharmacy's software from home. Pharmacists who are not on duty can work from home to complete phone appointments (shorter follow-ups) and clinical checks for chronic, non-urgent prescriptions that are forwarded to them from the dispensary. They can also review clinical patient information to prepare for their appointments. They should be reimbursed for these hours worked outside of the pharmacy. In addition, pharmacists at home would be on an on-call schedule to cover the dispensary pharmacist if they have an emergency. Note that if the pharmacist covering patient appointments had an emergency, appointments for that day could be cancelled and rescheduled for another day (or completed at home via phone or video calls) as it may be challenging for another pharmacist to cover appointments for patients that are not theirs.

Patients who see their pharmacist at their appointment would discuss which medications should be continued and which should be discontinued or followed up on with prescribers. The clinical pharmacist would then forward any medications that require refilling to the dispensary. These refills would be considered already clinically checked. The patient's medications would then be in the queue to be prepared and technically checked. Patients should have some supply of their medications on hand when they attend their appointments (i.e. their appointments should be scheduled at least one week before their medication refills are due) so there will be no pressure to prepare their medications on the same day of their appointment.

To reduce interruptions and to protect the integrity of prescriptions, it would be a legal requirement that all new prescriptions would come in via fax from prescribers only. No patients would be bringing in new prescriptions to the pharmacy. In other words, the only patients coming into the pharmacy are those who have an appointment with their clinical pharmacist, those picking up medications after they have received a phone call that they are ready, and those inquiring about over-the-counter (OTC) products. OTC questions can be addressed by the dispensary pharmacist, who should leave a note in the patient's file for their respective pharmacist indicating that they are starting a new OTC product.

The dispensary pharmacist would be positioned at the beginning of the pharmacy counter to complete an initial therapeutic check on new prescriptions. If there are urgent prescriptions which the patient will require the same day (e.g. for antibiotics), the staff will prepare the medication and deliver it or have it ready for pickup the same day. Otherwise, new prescriptions will be forwarded for a deeper therapeutic check by the pharmacists who cover the respective patients.

The following case will demonstrate the different ways a prescription could be reviewed and processed.

Let's say Pharmacist A is working in the dispensary for the month of April, and Pharmacists B and C will be covering appointments (Pharmacist B for the first two weeks of April, and Pharmacist C for the second two weeks). Each day, Pharmacist A will receive new prescriptions from prescribers, as well as refill requests from the other pharmacist on duty after each patient appointment. Pharmacist A will prioritize the prescriptions as they come in:

- <u>New prescriptions that are urgent</u>- Urgency is assessed and determined by the dispensary pharmacist (Pharmacist A). These will get checked and prepared for same-day delivery/ pick-up. These prescriptions take priority over all others. If the prescriptions are for patients in groups under Pharmacist B or C, Pharmacist A will still prepare them (as they are urgent) and forward a note to the respective pharmacist so they know the patient is taking a new medication. The clinical pharmacist (B or C) can review the new medication at home or at a later appointment and call the patient at a suitable time.

- <u>New prescriptions that are not urgent (e.g. those for chronic conditions)</u>- These will be flagged for the respective pharmacist's clinical review. Those belonging to patients in Pharmacist A's group can be reviewed by Pharmacist A during their dispensary shift or at a later time. Those belonging to patients in Pharmacist B's group will be forwarded to Pharmacist B and the same for Pharmacist C's patients. Pharmacists could have some scheduled time within their shifts to only review their respective new prescriptions. This could mean 30 minutes each day or every other day where the pharmacy does not schedule any patient appointments so that no refills are processed (these 30 minutes would be in addition to the 30 minutes of break time each pharmacist would be expected to take). Pharmacists working at home would be able to review and approve new prescriptions for preparation even if they are not physically working in the pharmacy that week. New prescriptions do not make up the majority of a pharmacy's workload in most cases, so the work from home would not be expected to overwhelm pharmacists. It would be up to the pharmacists how soon new non-urgent prescriptions should be prepared, as they might want to speak to patients or review clinical information before approving these new prescriptions. Pharmacists should communicate with prescribers if significant delays in starting therapy are expected, and should work together when monitoring and adjusting therapy.

- <u>Refills:</u> These would be forwarded to the pharmacy on the same day of a patient's appointment after they meet with their pharmacist. However, they would not be expected to be ready for the same day as the appointment. How soon the refills would be ready would depend on the pharmacy's workflow and the volume of priority prescriptions and other refills. Patients attending their appointment would be called to pick up their refills a few days or one week after the appointment or can have them delivered when ready.

For pharmacies with only one pharmacist and one registered technician on duty, the pharmacist would be responsible for covering appointments and completing clinical checks on new prescriptions. New prescriptions coming into the pharmacy would have to be flagged for the pharmacist to review, perhaps during their appointments, before they can be prepared by the dispensary team. Again, a note would also be forwarded to the patient's respective pharmacist to alert them that their patient has started a new therapy so they can perform a deeper clinical review.

In the Phresh Pharmacy, legislative changes would be required so that patients would not be able to fill different medications at different pharmacies. This will improve continuity of care. Furthermore, all pharmacists would be entitled to at least a 30 min break per 8-hour shift. In pharmacies with only one pharmacist on duty per shift, there would be no appointments and the dispensary would close when the pharmacist goes on break.

In terms of professional services, Medschecks or medication reviews would be completed daily as part of the pharmacist's job. This is how it should be - pharmacists should *always* be performing medication reviews to benefit patients - not only whenever they have the time. Therefore, patients and other insurance providers (other than the government) may have to participate in the payment for medication reviews as the volume of reviews per pharmacy would increase. Additional services (e.g. smoking cessation programs, immunizations) could be scheduled when patients are expected to have shorter appointments (e.g. a quick appointment to follow up on symptoms, lifestyle goals etc. when there are no medication or clinical changes). Pharmacies should be able to bill for these additional services the same way they currently do. Also, pharmacies would still charge a dispensing fee for every prescription they fill.

Conclusion

The key differences between a Phresh Pharmacy and the pharmacies that we currently work in are that a Phresh Pharmacy is organized, and decisions on whether and when prescriptions are processed are made entirely by the pharmacist. There is no pressure from patients or the business model to have prescriptions ready within a certain amount of time - the urgency is a clinical decision made by the pharmacist.

Instead of seeing the same patient three times in a given month for three different issues (e.g. once to get their medication filled, again to get their spouse's medication filled and a third time to get vaccinated), the pharmacist only reviews a patient once every three months to deal with all of their current and upcoming concerns.

A Phresh Pharmacy is proactive because it refills all of a patient's medications before they completely run out, and faxes the prescriber about clinical concerns before a patient starts a medication rather than in the middle of a course of therapy. This reduces interruptions, improves efficiency and allows pharmacists to work as clinicians. Another key difference is that the pharmacist has proper support in terms of staffing and this will increase pharmacist job satisfaction, allow pharmacists to take well-deserved breaks and have coverage for emergencies. Of course, it will also improve their ability to provide valuable clinical services to patients.

In addition to the legislative changes required for a Phresh Pharmacy, we must educate our patients that retail pharmacy involves clinical work that requires time to produce valuable health outcomes. It is not primarily a business where they pay for and pick up prescriptions and then head out the door. Patients need to know that pharmacists can do much more for them than just count their pills. Pharmacists just need the time and the right laws protecting them to be able to do so.

If we as a profession don't start to envision and implement changes, who else will do it for us? I am sure that any community pharmacist will say that change needs to happen in our profession - it is well-recognized. It is also well-recognized that the clinical role of a pharmacist should somehow be separate from the dispensing role. However, we now need to discuss *how* that change will happen. The details of what laws need to change, what pharmacist associations need to do to better support their pharmacists, and what restrictions pharmacy companies should face to change the business model, need to be discussed. I hope that this book will start these kinds of discussions. And above all, I hope that all community pharmacists will have the opportunity to practice in a Phresh Pharmacy someday.

References

Introduction

1. Ontario Ministry of Health. 2023. *Professional Pharmacy Services*. https://www.ontario.ca/page/professional-pharmacy-services

2. Ontario College of Pharmacists. 2021. *Clinical Viewers Now Available to All Community Pharmacies*. *https://pharmacyconnection.ca/clinical-viewers-now-available-to-all-community-pharmacies/*

3. Barrett, J. 2020. "2020 Pharmacy Salary Survey Results: Salaries Stabilize as Stress and Job Dissatisfaction Soar". *Drug Topics Journal* 164 (12). https://www.drugtopics.com/view/2020-pharmacy-salary-survey-results.

Chapter 1

4. Robinson, J. 2019. "Time constraints cause overwhelming distress for one in seven UK community pharmacists." *The Pharmaceutical Journal,* May 30, 2019. https://pharma-

ceutical-journal.com/article/news/time-con-
straints-cause-overwhelming-distress-for-one-
in-seven-uk-community-pharmacists-

5. Drug Topics. 2015. *Pharmacy Staffing Levels Can Threaten Patient Lives.* https://www.-drugtopics.com/view/pharmacy-staffing-lev-els-can-threaten-patient-lives

6. Gebhart, F. 2019. "Pharmacists Want More Time With Patients." *Drug Topics,* March 18, 2019. https://www.drugtopics.com/view/pharmacists-want-more-time-patients

7. Tariq, Rayhan, A., Rishik Vashisht, Ankur Sinha, and Yevgeniya Scherbak. 2023. "Medication Dispensing Errors and Prevention." *StatPearls Publishing,* May 2, 2023. https://www.ncbi.nlm.nih.gov/books/NBK519065/

8. Yande, S.D., Prajakta P. Masurkar, Suma Gopinathan, and Sujit S. Sansgiry. 2020. "A Naturalistic Observation Study of Medication Counseling Practices at Retail Chain Pharma-

cies." *Pharmacy Practice* 18, no. 1 (January - March):1696. https://doi.org/10.18549/PharmPract.2020.1.1696

9. Hanna, Maria. 2019. " The Patient Vs. The Clock: Time Constraints are Damaging Progress in Medicine." *in-Training,* September 23, 2019. https://in-training.org/the-patient-vs-the-clock-time-constraints-are-damaging-progress-in-medicine-18623

Chapter 2

10. Desselle, S.P. 2020. "Tip of the Week: Minimizing Pharmacy Workflow Interruptions." *Pharmacy Times.* https://www.pharmacy-times.com/view/tip-of-the-week-minimizing-pharmacy-workflow-interruptions

11. Sinclair, A., M. Slimm, and D. Terry. 2012. "To Investigate How Disruptive Interruptions are on Paediatric Dispensary Accuracy Checkers." *BMJ Archives of Disease In Childhood* 97: e17. https://adc.bmj.com/content/97/5/e17.1

12. Burford, M.E., A.E. Yeck, J.A. Tucker, L.M. Barker, and K.S. Pasupathy. 2011. "Stressors in the Pharmacy: An Observational Study of Interruptions." *Proceedings of the Human Factors and Ergonomics Society Annual Meeting,* 55(1): 1970 -1974. https://doi.org/ 10.1177/1071181311551411

13. Reddy, A., E. Abebe, A.J. Rivera, J.A. Stone, and M.A. Chui. 2019. "Interruptions in Community Pharmacies: Frequency, Sources, and Mitigation Strategies." *Research in Social and Administrative Pharmacy,* 15(10): 1243-1250. https://doi.org/10.1016/ j.sapharm.2018.10.030

14. Jacobs, S., K. Hassell, and S. Johnson. 2013. *Managing Workplace Stress to Enhance Safer Practice in Community Pharmacy: A Scoping Study.* https://pharmacyresearchuk.org/wp-content/uploads/2013/07/Final-report-FI-NAL.pdf

15. Ontario College of Pharmacists. 2022. *Prescription (Rx) Summary Regulation Chart.* https://www.ocpinfo.com/wp-content/uploads/2019/05/Prescription-Regulation-Summary-Chart-Summary-of-Laws.pdf

16. Ontario College of Pharmacists. 2023. *Pharmacist Prescribing: Initiating, Adapting and Renewing Prescriptions.* https://www.ocpinfo.com/practice-education/practice-tools/support-materials/technician-role/

Chapter 3

17. Ontario College of Pharmacists. 2024. *Operating a Lock & Leave.* https://www.ocpinfo.com/practice-education/opening-operating-pharmacy/lock-leave/

18. Ministry of Labour, Immigration, Training and Skills Development (Government of Ontario). 2023. *Your Guide to the Employment Standards Act - Hours of Work.* https://www.ontario.ca/document/your-guide-employment-standards-act-0/hours-work

19. Ministry of Labour, Immigration, Training and Skills Development (Government of Ontario). 2022. *Industries and Jobs with Exemptions or Special Rules - EMS, Healthcare and Health Professionals.* https://www.ontario.ca/document/industries-and-jobs-exemptions-or-special-rules/ems-healthcare-and-health-professionals#section-21

20. Ministry of Labour. 2017. *ESA Exemptions Toolkit: Pharmacists.* https://www.ocpinfo.com/library/news-and-alerts/download/ESA_Exemptions_Pharmacist_Toolkit.pdf

21. Ontario College of Pharmacists. 2017. *Exemptions and Exclusions Under the Employment Standards Act.* https://www.ocpinfo.com/consultation/exemptions-and-exclusions-employment-standards-act/

22. McKeen & Associates, P.C. 2021. *Nursing Fatigue Causes Medication Errors in Detroit.* https://www.mckeenassociates.com/articles/

126

nursing-fatigue-causes-medication-errors-in-detroit/

23. Balayssac, D., B. Pereira, J. Virot, C. Lambert, A. Collin, D. Alapini, J-M. Gagnaire, N. Authier, D. Cuny, and B. Vennat. 2017. "Work-Related Stress, Associated Comorbidities and Stress Causes in French Community Pharmacies: A Nation-Wide Cross-Sectional Study." *Peer J* 5, (October): e3973. https://doi.org/10.7717/peerj.3973

24. Peebles, A. 2022. "Overworked Pharmacy Employees are the COVID Pandemic's Invisible Victims." *Bloomberg,* January 26, 2022. https://www.bloomberg.com/news/articles/2022-01-26/overworked-pharmacy-employees-are-the-covid-pandemic-s-invisible-victims

25. Levy, S. 2022. "CVS Health to Give Pharmacists Dedicated Lunch Break." *Canadian Healthcare Network,* February 14, 2022. https://www.canadianhealthcarenetwork.ca/

cvs-health-give-pharmacists-dedicated-lunch-break?check_logged_in=1

Chapter 4

26. "Alert Fatigue." 2019. *Patient Safety Network,* September 7, 2019. https://psnet.ahrq.gov/primer/alert-fatigue

Chapter 5

27. Ontario College of Pharmacists. 2023. *Legal Scope of Practice & Authorized Acts for Pharmacy.* https://www.ocpinfo.com/wp-content/uploads/2019/05/Legal-Authority-Scopes.pdf

28. Pechlivanoglou, P., L. Abrahamyan, L. Mac-Keigan, G.P. Consiglio, L. Dolovich, P. Li, S.M. Cadarette, V.E. Rac, J. Shin, and M. Krahn. 2016. "Factors Affecting the Delivery of Community Pharmacist-Led Medication Reviews: Evidence from the MedsCheck Annual Service in Ontario." *BMC Health Services Research* 16, 666 (November). https://doi.org/10.1186/s12913-016-1888-2

29. Bain, K.T., H.M. Holmes, M.H. Beers, V. Maio, S. M. Handler, and S.G. Pauker. 2008. "Discontinuing Medications: A Novel Approach for Revising the Prescribing Stage of the Medication-Use Process." *Journal of the American Geriatrics Society* 56, no. 10 (September): 1946-1952. https://doi.org/10.1111/j.1532-5415.2008.01916.x

30. Glassdoor. 2015. *Pharmacy Manager Rexall Employee Review*. https://www.glassdoor.com/Reviews/Employee-Review-Rexall-RVW7215670.htm

Author Contact Information

I hope you enjoyed this book and that it benefited you in some way. Thank you for reading it.

My email is mwpharmacybusiness@gmail.com

My LinkedIn is

www.linkedin.com/in/mwpharmacy

I would love to discuss any ideas for the retail pharmacy industry and how to implement proper change to improve working conditions for pharmacists.